THE SECRETS TO AUDITIONING FOR COMMERCIALS

ON CAMERA WITH IRIS ACKER

ON CAMERA WITH IRIS ACKER

THE SECRETS TO AUDITIONING FOR COMMERCIALS

by

Iris Acker

dp

DISTINCTIVE PUBLISHING CORP.

Library of Congress Cataloging-in-Publication Data

Acker, Iris Y., date.
   The secrets to auditioning for commercials   /   by Iris Y. Acker.
     p.   cm.
   ISBN 0-942963-04-0
     1. Television broadcasting--Auditions.   2. Acting for television-
-Vocational guidance.   3. Television advertising--Vocational
guidance.   I. Title.
PN1992.8.A3A35   1991   90-20427
791.45'028'023--dc20   CIP

THE SECRETS TO AUDITIONING FOR COMMERCIALS
By Iris Y. Acker
Copyright 1991 by Iris Y. Acker
Produced by Ratzlaff & Associates
Cover and Illustrations by Therese Cabell
Published by Distinctive Publishing Corp.
P.O. Box 17868
Plantation, FL 33318-7868

Printed in the United States of America

Price $9.95

Dedicated to a "good friend"

GLORIA GONZALEZ

Only with her encouragement and expertise
has this book been written.

CONTENTS

INTRODUCTION

I watch television. A lot. I'm not partial to the news, sports, movies or sitcoms. That's just the stuff that fills the air while I wait for . . . the commercials!

While most viewers use this time to go to the refrigerator or hem a pair of slacks . . . I watch the commercials and listen intently, many times making notes on the script and performance.

Why?

Because that's how I make my living. I appear often in commercials which are telecast all over the country. I teach a very successful course in "Auditioning for Commercials," and it is through my students and their insistence that I've decided to share my "secrets" with you; the secrets of how to get paid to sell someone else's products.

Being a commercial actress has its definite fringe benefits:

1. The money is great.
2. The exposure to film-making is exciting. (The same techniques employed in a multimillion dollar feature film are also at work in the production of a commercial.)
3. You enjoy a high visibility as people on the street remember you from a recent commercial.

4. You often are working with the top creative and technical people in the field; valuable contacts which could later lead elsewhere.
5. More than one "overnight success" has emerged after a successful, long-running commercial.
6. It's hard work — but it's fun!

Before I started teaching my class, it occurred to me that, by comparison with many of my contemporaries, I was getting more than my fair share of commercials. Not that they weren't as talented or as "right" or as lucky. In many cases, they were much more suited for the particular commercial than I was, yet I wound up getting hired and the commercial rewritten to suit me.

Why?

Because after years of studying the specialized craft of commercials and all its aspects, I realized that I had "secrets" that they didn't share in.

It is these same secrets that I will divulge as you continue to read . . .

Be patient.

The "magic" doesn't happen overnight. So settle back, read, and be prepared to absorb what it has taken me years to learn.

You'll never switch a commercial "off" again.

PROLOGUE

Several years ago I was sent on a commerical audition and given the number 48. At that time, all actors would be given the same audition time and you just waited your turn, or as in this case, we were all herded into a huge room and listened to each other read. (See where the term "cattle call" constantly pertains to auditions.)

Screen Actor's Guild has eliminated all of the above; but that "cattle call" was a blessing in disguise for me. After hearing and watching the 47 actors who preceded me, I realized I had a secret — the secret of auditioning. And they did not.

When it was my turn, I gambled, and on camera said, "I'm number 48 and everyone after me is an imitation." I read the commercial while another 48 actors who were to follow listened. I was "called back" and got the commercial.

I got the audition with a "check-in" call to the agent who said, "Iris, I'm casting a commercial, but you're not really right for it. You're too old for the young mother and not old enough for the grandmother." I asked to please be sent anyway. She did. They rewrote the commercial for me.

When we were shooting that commercial, the director complimented me on the great job I was doing on the TV series I was in and how lucky for them I happened to be in New York now to do this commercial. I don't know who they thought I was. I have learned to say thanks to any compliment, mine or not, and to smile and nod my head a lot without saying anything. I happen to look like a lot of people and like a lot of working actresses.

I hope you do, too, as it can only help.

In this book, I share my secrets with you. It's not magic — simply a formula that has worked very successfully for me. (I recently purchased a 37' sailboat for my husband and me, with payments from commercials and residuals and a little continued assistance from the Credit Union.)

In addition to the proper dress attire, I discuss how to analyze the script, how to read to a camera, how to read when there is no camera, how to prepare an audition when there is no script, and the importance of your pictures and a resume. What you should and should not say can either get you an audition or "kill" it for you. You've got to GET the audition before you GET the commercial.

I teach a class in "How To Audition For Commercials," and at my students' urgings, I have written this book. They tell me no other teacher has been able to communicate the success of commercial auditioning as well as I have. I believe them, because everything I teach I have done, and it's won me many, many commercials — which I purposely will not name.

Under the heading on your resume of commercials, I always suggest you put "list on request" as I do. If I listed all the commercials I've done, and a "Pepsi" appeared, "Coca-Cola" would never use me. It wouldn't matter if I had done the "Pepsi" ten years ago, if "Coca-Cola" sees it on my resume, I'm dead. All you're obligated to tell are your recent conflicts, and they change from month to month — so why list them and constantly have to redo your resume?

I think the most important parts of this book are the intimate details of commercial auditions, which I don't hesitate to share with you. Yes, there is a definite technique of handling the casting director's direction, "Be natural, just be yourself."

As you know, an agent or a casting director can be either male or female. I will alternate my references, using "he" or "she" for a chapter.

I use the term "they" often. It pertains to anyone who does casting.

A talent agent represents actors for a commission of 10%. A casting director represents the client or an advertising agency or a production company. They are salaried or self-employed. When casting a commercial, the casting director calls the agent for the talent needed.

If you will accept auditioning for commercials as a challenge and *ATTACK* it as such, you will win and enjoy it at the same time.

CHAPTER 1

PREPARING FOR THE AUDITION

THE AUDITION
begins at home, with the phone call from the agent telling
you where to go, what time to be there, what the product is,
and confirming that you don't have a conflict.

HOPEFULLY,
the agent will give you a lot more information than that. She
will tell you the character you're supposed to be and approx-
imate age category.

FOR EXAMPLE,
she might say, "You're a housewife, between thirty and
thirty-five years old." She'll tell you if it's a kitchen scene, a
barbecue, on the street, in the bedroom, etc., etc. Or she
might say, "Be yourself . . ." Let's talk about that phrase.

BE YOURSELF
. . . never take offense when they say that. Of course, they
haven't the vaguest idea what you're really like. You know
that, I know that, and it isn't what they really mean. It's a clue,
telling you you're expected to be like all the other guys and
gals on TV who portray the characters the agent just told you

you're going to audition as, the housewife, the gas station attendant, the bank executive. What it really means is that physically either the agent or casting director who has seen your picture thinks you fit the part of the housewife, the gas station attendant, the bank executive, etc., etc., so go on looking that way, meaning the stereotyped ones you have already seen on commercials countless times.

They are not looking for change. They want you to imitate. They want you to be exactly like the people who are already doing commercials. If they want any change, they will let you know. They'll say, "We're looking for someone 'far out', a real kooky character," or, "This is a change of pace for Proctor & Gamble," or whatever the product or the advertising agency might be.

ONE OF YOUR BEST TEACHERS
is your TV set. If you want to do commercials, even if you hate watching the programs, watch the commercials. Listen to the copy and watch the actors.

No matter how much better you think you can do it, or how much better you think you can write it, the audition you go to will probably be written very similarly and the person they're looking for, if she is physically you, means you're an "in" type, and that's in your favor.

IF YOU'RE LUCKY,
the agent has given you at least the amount of information that I just mentioned. If not, it's up to you to ask the right questions of her:
  1. Who am I?
  2. How old am I?
  3. What's the location? Is it an indoor or outdoor scene?
Then it's up to you to dress properly. Try to get as close as possible to what the character would be wearing on the

actual commercial

> Bank executive: suit, shirt and tie.
>
> Gas station attendant: casual shirt and pants, and perhaps a cap.
>
> Housewife: skirt and blouse or a simple shirtwaist dress. (Most housewives on TV commercials do not wear pants.)

Yes, I know you wear jeans at home, but don't wear them to the audition, because they don't wear them on "the shoot" (when you film the commercial).

Gals, please, always wear stockings and appropriate shoes. Even though you may only be taped from the waist up, the client or the director may be present, and you should be perfectly groomed for the best impression.

If you show up looking like, or dressed as, the character in the commercial, they'll appreciate your interest and they'll appreciate your making it easier for them to see how you would look dressed as a housewife, a bank executive, plumber, etc. You stand more of a chance.

You can do it suggestively. (You don't have to walk around in a clown outfit or plumber's clothes.) Take the outfit with you and put it on at the audition.

You have to be willing to make a fool of yourself. The world of commercials, film and theater is very similar. It gives us a chance to play "let's pretend" for the rest of our lives. It allows us to be children forever. To live out someone's fantasies — but at the same time it gives us the opportunity to use the talent we have in portraying many different characters. It also means that if you really want that job, you've got to be willing to make a fool of yourself. The financial rewards can make it all worthwhile.

I have been Mrs. Santa Claus (in a gray wig and makeup aging me twenty years), a haggard housewife in a mop commercial, as well as a glamorous dowager in a long gown, resplendent with jewels, and yes, I "dressed" that way for each of the auditions.

I wore a gray wig and "granny" glasses for the Mrs. Santa Claus audition; messy hair, a housedress and no makeup for the haggard housewife; and a long gown, long gloves and a tiara for the wealthy dowager.

I was recently sent on a girdle audition and told to be myself. I asked if I was to look overweight. The agent said no. "They" had seen my picture and requested me. When I got to the audition and saw the other women waiting and read the copy, I realized my "full face" picture was deceiving and, although my body was thin, they were expecting a "chubby."

Willing to "make a fool of myself," I went to the ladies room and wrapped a roll of toilet tissue over my body and stuffed several paper towels in the proper places. I thought I now looked pleasingly and believably plump.

It was a two-minute commercial and the script was long and difficult. I obviously read well, because I was called back and told I could leave the lumps off. They had rewritten the copy for me.

The eight people who witnessed my audition laughed at my failed and obvious attempt to look fat, then realized how I certainly deserved another chance for my effort and excellent reading.

I did that commercial looking like myself and I had the last laugh.

CHAPTER 2

AUDITIONING WITH SIMPLE COPY

Always try to arrive at the audition at least a half hour before your "call," in plenty of time to look at the script. Sign in and . . . *GET A SCRIPT!*

1. Always ask at the audition if there is a "storyboard." A storyboard is a series of pictures in boxes with the words the actor will be saying, telling the story of the commercial. (See page 117.)

    If there is a storyboard, it can only help you. Study it carefully. What is your character wearing? What prop is he using? What are his actions?

    An artist has taken a lot of time drawing the pictures of the characters and the action. The artist drew exactly what the writer suggested. The closer you can come as an actor to fulfilling the writer's and the artist's choices, the closer you will come to getting the commercial. Usually there is a script in addition to the storyboard. Look at the storyboard, but read from the script.

2. Verify product name and pronunciation of it.

3. Make sure you're pronouncing *ALL* words correctly. (If in doubt, ask someone — another actor, the receptionist.)

4. Don't ask the casting director, the director, or the client inside the casting room. It's too late. You must rehearse, saying the words correctly. Those casting mustn't know that you don't know everything.

5. The most important part of preparing for your audition is NOW! You must say the copy OUT LOUD, whether it's one word, one line, or ten lines. Sitting in the reception room reading the copy to yourself silently or moving your lips or just thinking it and saying it to yourself won't do. This holds true for the beginner as well as the advanced.

You have to say it out loud so you hear your own voice. If you wait until you get inside when you're going to do the actual audition, the sound of your own voice will frighten you because it isn't at all the way you will have planned to have said it when you were just thinking it or moving your lips. It's amazing how different it is when you actually say it than when you think it or just move your lips, thinking you're saying it.

If you feel uncomfortable saying it out loud in the reception room where everyone else is waiting to audition, go to the lavatory, go out in the hall or out in the street, but say it *OUT LOUD.*

Sometimes you arrive early or are just on time and they'll say, "Go right in. There's nobody else here. Here's the copy and let's go." Don't do it. Don't go in. Don't let them convince you to go right in without reading that script out loud, outside. Plead diarrhea, severe cramps, lost your wallet, anything! Be prepared with something and don't go in until you have read that script out loud, several times. Make sure you're saying the product name correctly. Ask the receptionist to say it. Verify the correct pronunciation of any word you're not sure of.

I don't know how many auditions you go on, or will be

going on, but every one should be important enough for you to dress properly and prepare vocally and physically. This is a business. Your business. Don't allow yourself to be intimidated by "them." You take charge. Be assertive. Be sure. Be pleased by the way you sound.

Next: Analyze the script. Make certain decisions —how to analyze the product name without shouting it; where to "color" the copy so that it sounds believable, natural; and finally, where the "tag" of the commercial starts. It generally is the last line or the last two lines, or sometimes, just an action.

The tag: (Generally) should be done differently from the rest of the commercial. It sums it up. Or it has nothing to do with the commercial. It may be humorous. It tells the viewing audience the commercial is over. When it's an action, it may be a wife poking her husband with her elbow, a crinkled nose, or a wink.

Here are some short commercials. Take notice of the "tag."

Woman: "I always thought coffee was coffee. That the method you used or the pot you used made the difference. Then I discovered Coffeola. It's got a deeper, richer flavor."

Tag: "But the aroma alone says, 'drink me.'"

Man: "Who said a man's cologne can't be different? Whoever said it never tried La Differencia. The man's cologne that dares . . . So masculine, yet so tempting."

Tag: "Daring and different. That's why we call it 'La Differencia.'"

Read them out loud and see what you would do with the tag. Again, watch the commercials on TV. Look for and listen for the tag. A pause before the tag, for emphasis, helps.

REVIEWING
1. Color the copy.
2. Pause before the tag.
3. Make the point of the commercial. (Sell the product.)
4. Be distinctive, a little bit different, staying within the realm of believability. Never be outlandish, unless they specifically ask you to be.
5. Memorize the first and last line and hold the copy so that you don't bob your head up and down when reading.

Practice in front of a mirror. Don't block your face with the script. Hold it comfortably, not to the side, not too low or too high.

If you're so nervous that the paper shakes, hold it with two hands or back it with a manila envelope or a clipboard. Use your mirror as a camera (painful as it is). If you don't see yourself too often in the mirror, you're not looking up enough. Try using your thumb as a guide, moving it on to the next line to find the place quickly. Whatever technique will work for you, practice it so you'll be at ease.

When you go inside for the taping, assume the client and the director, as well as the casting director, will be there. They may not be — but be prepared to *BE* the character in the commercial from the moment you enter the audition room because they will want to believe the actor they hire really is the person in that commercial. They want to feel that you're like that all the time.

Even a "name" like Nancy Walker, in the client's eyes, is seen only as the diner waitress who uses "Bounty" towels. A Bill Cosby with "Jell-O," or any other name identified with a product, has created an image that has convinced the consumer and the client.

Well, you're an unknown. Yet, I know they want to feel, when you walk into that room, "There she is." They're thinking you're *PHYSICALLY* right for it, so be up and smiling and ready to put them at ease. Believe me, they're more nervous than you are. For you, it will be just another audition, but for the advertising agency, their future with the client depends on the commercial.

The director's claim to do any more commercials for these people is at stake.

So, be at ease and comfortable, and as much like the character as possible, whether she's a bouncy housewife or a cranky auto mechanic. Enter as you will be in the commercial — so they can discover you.

If no one introduces you, introduce yourself. If there's only a technician or casting director running the camera, keep the same attitude. If there's a tech booth (a small room, behind glass, where the technicians operating can be seen, with room for a few to sit and watch), you never know who will be in it.

If you've analyzed the script really well, really do look exactly as they picture, read "as you've been taught," you've got that commercial. I'm sure you know if you're an "in" commercial type, because you're watching TV and the commercials and you see actors who look like you.

When you enter the audition room, go to your "mark." The mark can be a piece of tape on the floor, a chalk mark, anything that will signify where they want you to stand so that you'll be heard on the microphone and positioned right for the camera.

Don't ask, "How do you want me to read this commercial?" They assume that you are professional enough to know how the commercial should be read. In fact, they may not know how they want it done. They may only have some vague ideas, and hopefully, they tell you about them before you read. Some clues, for example: "She's up and cheery," "He's grumpy until he tries our product, then he smiles."

Too often, they will not say anything. While you were in the reception room going over the script, you have made several decisions already. When you go inside, either no one will give you direction and right or wrong, you can only go with your instincts (after analyzing the script), or they will give you direction which may be the exact opposite of the way you have chosen to do it. You have no alternative but to do it *THEIR* way. You'll have to make an instant transition.

Of course, it couldn't hurt to rehearse it several different ways, just in case. Ask yourself, "How else can I do it? What can I do with this copy that's distinctive, that's me?"

After I do the commercial their way, if I have an alternate choice prepared, I ask if I may do another "take" another way, and by doing so still get my choice on tape. This has worked for me, where they have used me and my way of delivery.

At one audition, the copy said "spokeswoman" at the top. After reading the script, I got this gut feeling of what would really work, what would sell this product. Sure enough, when I got inside, they reminded me it was straight spokeswoman — right to the camera. I did it their way, and when it was over I asked if I could do it again, another way. They asked what I had in mind. I told them the words were very comfortable to say, only it would be easier to say them as if it was a great big secret, almost as if I was on the telephone telling my best friend about this product — but "don't tell anyone else." They let me try it. (Generally they'll say yes, because they're always interested in ideas. Many times you can change their minds.)

When you do this, you gamble. They can buy your idea, but not you. They'll use another actor, and there's nothing you can do about it. The first time I tried this, I got the commercial. The second time I didn't, but they used my concept anyway. I still choose to gamble. You can change their minds, but do it their way first.

When you are reading the copy, endow the camera with a face. It must become a living person. Talk to your best friend or someone you can confide in. If you use that "delivery," that approach, you should be "right on." (Excluding comedic or outlandish copy.) But when they're looking for real people, when they're asking you to be yourself, use this technique.

Be sure to ask for a rehearsal, in a positive manner. "May I have a rehearsal?" or "Rehearsal please?"

When you read from a script, hold the copy so you don't block your face, but high enough so only your eyes go up and down the paper, not your whole head.

When you rehearse, do not slate your name. You simply do the commercial or read the copy as if you were being taped.

When you rehearse, they'll photograph you on the TV monitor, but won't be taping. Most often, after rehearsing, they'll have suggestions for the taping, such as, "Not bad, but you could be happier," or "Very good, but you're too happy." Only by rehearsing will you get an opinion before you're taped.

When they are taping, you will be asked to "stand by" and on "action" to please slate your name. It's perfectly acceptable to say, "Hi, my name is . . . ," or "Hello, I'm . . ." Take a beat before you start reading. Don't make your name part of the commercial.

Count to three and slate your name IN CHARACTER. You entered "in character," so carry through with your name and then into the script.

If they ask for a voice level, start reading the script until they stop you. Never say, "Testing, one, two, three . . ." Again, it's the professional thing to do.

Okay, now we're back to that "mark."

They're going to ask you to slate your name and go. (The

word slate actually refers to a small board held in front of an actor shooting a commercial. It has the director's name, the product and which "take" written on it. At an audition, it's just a synonym for "say.") It's up to you at this point to ask for a rehearsal. When you rehearse, do not slate you name. You simply do the commercial, or read the copy as if you were being taped.

After taping your audition, ask if you can see it. If they'll play it back for you and you feel you can really do better or you can correct some wrong physical motion, ask to do it again. Simply say, "I can do better. Please, let's tape it again."

THIS FORM MUST BE
FILLED OUT IN INK

COMMERCIAL PERFORMERS:
► Print your name.
► Print agent's name.
► Circle applicable interview.

EXHIBIT E
SAG / AFTRA
COMMERCIAL AUDITION REPORT   PAGE_____ OF_____

TO BE COMPLETED BY CASTING DIRECTOR				
(X) WHERE APPLICABLE TELEVISION □	ON CAMERA □	OFF CAMERA □	RADIO □	AUDITION DATE
INTENDED USE	UNION: SAG □ AFTRA □	Person to whom correspondence concerning this form shall be sent: (Name & Phone Number)		
CASTING REPRESENTATIVE NAME	COMMERICAL TITLE - NAME & NUMBER			ADVERTISER NAME
PRODUCT	JOB NUMBER	ADVERTISING AGENCY AND CITY		PRODUCTION COMPANY

INSTRUCTIONS: Circle the name of performer hired if known.   Mail one copy to SAG OR AFTRA on the 1st and 15th of each month.

NAME (PLEASE PRINT)	SOCIAL SECURITY NUMBER	AGENT (PLEASE PRINT)	ACTUAL CALL	TIME IN	TIME OUT	INITIAL	CIRCLE INTERVIEW NUMBER	SEX (X) M F	AGE (X) +40 -40	ETHNICITY (X) AP B C LH I	PWD (X)
							1st 2nd 3rd 4th				
							1st 2nd 3rd 4th				
							1st 2nd 3rd 4th				
							1st 2nd 3rd 4th				
							1st 2nd 3rd 4th				
							1st 2nd 3rd 4th				
							1st 2nd 3rd 4th				
							1st 2nd 3rd 4th				
							1st 2nd 3rd 4th				
							1st 2nd 3rd 4th				
							1st 2nd 3rd 4th				
							1st 2nd 3rd 4th				
							1st 2nd 3rd 4th				
							1st 2nd 3rd 4th				

This recorded audition material will not be used as a client demo, an audience reaction commercial, for copy testing or as a scratch track without payment of the minimum compensation provided for in the Commercials Contract and shall be used solely to determine the suitability of the performer for a specific commercial.
AUTHORIZED REPRESENTATIVE SIGNATURE_____

The only reason for requesting information on ethnicity, sex, age, and disability is for the talent unions to monitor applicant flow. The furnishing of such information is on a VOLUNTARY basis. The Authorized Representative's signature on this form shall not constitute a verification of the information supplied by performers.

Asian/Pacific — AP   Latino/Hispanic — L
Black — B   Native American — I
Caucasian — C   Performer with Disability — PWD

EXE / 8

Print your name so that it is legible. *Actual call* is the time your agent told you to be there. *Time in* is the time you actually arrive. Make sure you sign out when you leave, and initial at that time.

CHAPTER 3

AUDITIONING WITH AUDIO-VISUAL COPY

If you are given copy with audio and visual on the page:

Mother Magee's Macaroni

VIDEO	AUDIO
MCU of girl at department store counter.	And now ladies, step right up to the counter and watch me almost cook macaroni.
Dissolve to live display. Macaroni in a pot. Empty Mother Magee's Macaroni box next to it.	Yes, I said almost. How can I say otherwise when you use Mother Magee's?
Cut to CU of Mother Magee's Macaroni box on counter.	You simply empty the box into the pot,
Pan to pot with macaroni in it.	and watch it cook.

Cut to girl at counter holding box, then dolly back to include background of store.	Or, I should say, almost cook. With Mother Magee's Macaroni.

Read all the visual direction as well as the audio. Be aware of what the actor is doing while he is saying the lines, and whenever possible, do it. Hold up the product or brush teeth or scour sink, etc. Hold the product close to your face.

If you have the product of the commercial at home, take it to use in case they don't have it. I once took a can of scouring powder, and they begged me to leave it for the others auditioning. I did, but I put my name all over it.

When you get copy without visual direction, do as little as possible. Before we "take class" or are *TOLD* otherwise, we tend to overdo, especially theater actors. We use bad TV habits. The very same action we use on a stage can kill us on television.

1. Do you bob your head up and down? (Saying "yes" all the time?)

2. Do you overdo your head so that it goes side to side out of the frame? Are you talking with your hands? (We are generally taped from the waist up, sometimes just the neck up.)

3. Your *EYES* are the most important part of your face. Expressive eyes can win you a commercial. Use them. Be careful not to frown with your eyebrows; some of us "think" with our brows. It's not a pleasant look. Talk with your eyes. Relate to the camera with your eyes, intimately or comedically.

4. Do you open your mouth too much? Not enough?

5. Do you *SMILE*? Show your teeth — smile, smile.

Memorize a commercial and do it to your mirror several times. Each time, check for just one thing.

Do I bob my head?

Do I sway?

Am I using my mouth well?

Am I using my eyes? How about my eyebrows?

Am I talking with my hands?

Do I smile? Am I pleasant?

When you have finished reading the copy at the audition, be aware — the tape is probably still rolling. Don't editorialize. Don't make faces showing your dissatisfaction with your performance. Stay with the character until you're positive the machine is off. Then ask the casting director if you can do it over, if you goofed.

If, in the second or third line of copy, you goof, and it's not that bad, just keep on going. If it's really outlandish, stop. Then, in character, say, "I'm going to start from the top again." And do just that.

CHAPTER 4

AUDITIONING WHEN THERE IS NO CAMERA

The procedure is initially the same. You have your script in the reception room. You memorize the first and last lines. Remember to be "in character" the moment you enter the audition room. If they don't tell you where to stand to read, pick a favorable area opposite them.

Here is where the biggest dilemma arises. There's no camera. Who do you look at when you're reading? I suggest you pick out the friendliest face, anyone who ventured a smile, who looked as if they liked you. You won't know who anyone is and it doesn't matter. They rarely introduce themselves and they certainly won't add, "She's the script girl, he's the art director, she's the creative director, etc.," so go ahead and read to your choice.

You must use that person as if they were the camera. Your eyes to their eyes. Let everyone else in the room watch you. When you have finished reading (the same as if you were on camera), wait for a comment. It may be "Thank you, send the next actor in," or they may give you further direction, such as, "Faster, slower, sweeter, angrier, happier, sadder, etc.," and you get the chance to read again.

Listen very carefully to their direction, and do exactly as they ask.

If there isn't any script, you'll know that. Still dress for the commercial and enter in character and stay in character for the interview. Be prepared to pantomime if it's an athletic casting (tennis, golf, skiing).

Keep your ears open in the reception room. Listen to what the exiting actors say. Their comments can help. I got a commercial because I overheard an actress say to the receptionist, "If they wanted a comedienne, why didn't they say so." I quickly reread the very un-funny script and tried to inject humor wherever I could. I entered and used whatever comedy I could muster in the introductions. They did not give any direction, but I read the commercial humorously. They told me I was the first and only actress who read correctly.

CHAPTER 5

CUE CARDS

If you're reading from cue cards, big cards with the commercial copy printed on them in big letters, don't keep looking back at the camera. Use the cue card as you would the camera. Treat the card with the same intensity.

The cue card either surrounds the camera, is under it, or on either side.

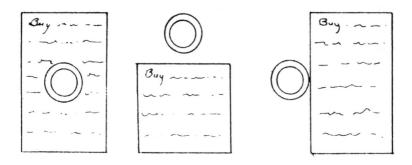

1.   If the cue card is beneath the camera, keep your chin up and your eyes wide in preparation for the bottom line.

2.   When it's on the side or when it surrounds the camera, just read the card as if it were the camera.

3.   Slate your name to the camera and try to finish and freeze to the camera.

AUDITIONING WITH A "TELEPROMPTER"

The script rolls from bottom to top on a machine placed or held above or below the lens of the camera. An arrow generally marks the line you are reading. The letters on the prompter are about 1/2 inch high.

Use the prompter as you would cue cards. In other words, relate to it as if it were the camera. Since it keeps rolling, the center will always be in the same place. But do relate. Endow the prompter as you would the camera. Warm eye contact is the keynote. Ask for a rehearsal, as you would if you were holding copy or reading cue cards.

When you are shooting a commercial with a lot of copy, a teleprompter is almost always used.

CHAPTER 6

ONE-LINERS

I personally hate "one-liners." I always feel the more I have to say, the better chance I have of getting it "right." But, on many commercials, the actor only gets to say one line.

For example: "Wow, that's wonderful!"

or   "That rag is dirty!"

or   "This orange juice has more pulp!"

In looking over my reel, I realized about half of my commercials were just "one-liners." Very often, I just said the "tag."

Thinking back on how I got those commercials, I realized, most often, I was asked to say that "one line" about three different ways. They usually give SOME direction.

For example: Very snooty, or very laid back, or with a lot of energy.

Then, they may add: "You can do it a couple of other ways, if you like." If the line is "Wow, that's wonderful," they do not mean, "WOW, that's wonderful," or "Wow, THAT'S wonderful," or "Wow, that's WONDERFUL," but literally three different ways.

I suggest you make a list of emotions.

Sincerity

Love

Sexiness

Anger

Suspicion

Joy

Excitement

Disappointment

Etc., etc., etc.

And while you're rehearsing, refer to your list, trying all your favorite emotions.

Some of the "one-liners" I've done on commercials are:

"That's nice."   A wife admiring her husband's art work.

They suggested sincere. I did it that way and then with love and admiration, almost whispered, and that's the one they used.

"Nonsense."   At a garden party. A haughty lady's answer to the butler's announcement that it will be raining soon.

"I'll take that one."   A mother handpicking shrimp for dinner.

"It's that Dade Savings difference."

"Twice the prints, twice the fun."

Above all, whenever possible, add humor!

CHAPTER 7

WHEN YOU HAVE TO EAT
AND DRINK ON CAMERA

It's all in the eyes . . .

How else can you express the joy of the food or drink, while chewing or swallowing?

Talk to yourself. Say what you're thinking, with your eyes.

For example: (think)

FOR DRINKS: I *LOVE* the flavor.

It's *SOOOO* cool.

This really warms me.

FOR FOOD, WHILE CHEWING: I *LOVE* the taste.

It's *SOOOO* delicious.

Notice the repetition of the word love. Whenever we say love, our eyes reflect it, show it, and are at their most expressive. Look in the mirror and try it.

Try using the list of "emotions" you use for "one-liners" as well: sexiness, joy, excitement, and always love. Most of all, before you eat and before you drink, express anticipation so that we'll know whether it will be hot or cold, and definitely tasty. After drinking, express satisfaction facially.

When drinking, instead of to the camera, face 3/4 or profile, so your face can be seen, not the bottom of the cup or can.

Notes

CHAPTER 8

COMBINATIONS AND IMPROVISATIONS

If you are reading with another actor, whether it be a husband-and-wife scene, two friends, a salesman and customer, etc., read to each other, not to the camera (unless you are specifically directed otherwise). Look at him while *HE'S* reading and react accordingly.

Hopefully, the actor you are reading with has also arrived early. Grab him and invite him into the hallway to rehearse your lines *TOGETHER*. This can definitely benefit both of you.

If it's an on-camera audition, be sure to ask for a rehearsal. Try to stand in a three-quarter position (almost fourth position in ballet, or what theater actors call a "cheat" position).

If the script is directed to the viewing audience, look at your partner when he's talking, not at your script.

If it's two gals talking or two guys, be sure you're familiar with both parts. Even though the agent is specific on which role is yours, very often the casting director will ask you to switch parts.

You each slate your name and agent to the camera as directed by the casting director.

If you're not asked to "switch" roles, but would like to try the other part, ask.

It's generally easier to audition with another actor, having a person to relate to instead of a camera.

When there is no script, if they do not ask you to tell them "a little about yourself," they may ask for an improvisation.

Dictionary translation: To invent, to compose or recite without preparation.

They're looking for expression and creativeness. Usually there's a voice-over, while the actors pantomime the situation in a very natural, believable manner.

I did several commercials that I got through improvising and wound up "talking" as the result of my inventiveness.

In an airline commercial, I'm rowing to Europe with my husband, our dog, lots of food and paper products filling the rowboat. The voice-over is saying, "Cheap is cheap, but with Air _____, we can fly to Europe" . . . etc., etc.

The audition was an improvisation of me being very bossy, showing my meek husband the way to Europe, using maps, the wind, the sun, etc. (By the way, they never asked if I could row a boat.) I remember adding lines at the audition, like, "We should have taken Mama. She'd love the salt air." When I shot the commercial, they asked me to add that line and several more.

Here are some sample improvisations. Try them.

For: Mr. Henry's Hamburgers

You're driving your kid brother home from summer camp. He hated to leave. He's on the verge of tears, not seeing his camp friends and not having camp activities any more . . . You try to cheer him up . . . nothing works . . . You finally spot a Mr. Henry's restaurant, point it out, offer to stop, and his big grin is your answer.

For: Sink Helper Dishwashers

You're shopping for Mother's Day in an appliance store for a dishwasher. A salesman is showing you several models. You find fault with them all, until you spot the "Sink Helper" dishwasher which has all the features Mother will love.

For: Thirsty Cola

You're nervously dressing for graduation. The viewing audience will assume it's your child's graduation. But as you primp and fuss and dress, you see your reflection in the mirror in "cap and gown," as your child walks in and hands you a "Thirsty Cola." He has the lines, "Here, Mom (or Dad), you look wonderful. I'm so proud of you. Let's drink to it!" (You embrace and then drink.)

CHAPTER 9

"TELL ME A LITTLE ABOUT YOURSELF"

When there isn't any script at an interview or taping, you'll often hear the casting director say, "In the absence of a script (which has yet to be written, or because the character doesn't talk in this spot), just tell us a little about yourself."

To be hit with this unexpectedly is generally a disaster. What the actor then says is generally too long, too many "uhs," not interesting, uncoordinated, and isn't going to get him the job.

Very often, they'll say, "Just tell us all the commercials you've done, plays and films you've been in. You know, just a brief resume." Boring!

If you get up and say, "Well, I did a Pepsi, uh, in, uh, January, and, uh, I did a showcase of "Waiting for Godot," uh, and a bit on *L.A. Law*," who cares?

Instead, be prepared with a one-minute or less "bio" that is interesting, unique, shows your personality and also sounds like you just thought it up. Here's your chance to act.

For example (when taped):

"Hi, I'm Iris Acker. I've spent every penny I've earned in this crazy, wonderful world of show business on a brand new 37-foot sailboat. As soon as we finish shooting this commercial, I'm off to the Bahamas. Anyone want to crew?"

Or: "My name is Nancy Raffa and I live in a zoo with my husband and four children. We have two dogs, a cat, a hamster, a parakeet, two aquariums filled with fish, two rabbits, several turtles, and a constant migration of red ants. We've all managed to work in commercials one time or another, especially the ants, who wouldn't be without me. It's just about feeding time . . . Sure, you're welcome, too."

Or: "Hi, I'm Cantillon Brasington. I'm not an Italian dish. It's my grandmother's name and my daughter's name and we're going to keep using it until somebody says it right."

Or: "Hello, I'm John Grout and I'm flying. As a matter of fact, I'm the youngest commercial pilot in the United States. I posed for a National Airlines ad in full pilot regalia and have been in show biz' ever since. You should hear my announcements to the passengers from the cockpit now."

Or: "Hi, I'm Brian Caits and I come from a theatrical family who did everything they could to discourage my entering the entertainment field. They paid for seven years of schooling in business administration for me, and the day I graduated I started making the 'rounds' of theatrical agents, who convinced me I could repay my family in about thirty years in this business. Two years down, twenty-eight to go. When it's in your blood . . ."

In every one of you there is something unique. You moonlight as a detective, a gourmet cook, a designer. Tie it into show biz: "When I'm not performing . . .," or ". . . in my spare time . . .," or "Between engagements . . ." We all know you're an actor; your agent wouldn't have sent you otherwise.

Sometimes your prepared "bio" may be adverse to the product. You're told you're a funny housewife and it's a kitchen scene. If in reality you moonlight as a private detective, I wouldn't tell the auditioners that. Don't gamble on their image of you being anything but a housewife in the kitchen. Prepare a brief improvisation you can do in character, not necessarily using the product or even mentioning the product.

I once used the following monologue when asked to be a funny housewife. "Hi, guys, I'm Iris Acker. I'm really thrilled to be here, but I'm in kind of a rush. I left dinner cooking on the stove. Shrimp fried rice. My recipe? I use a five minute rice, add chopped onion which I fry in oil with chopped green pepper. I add a couple of scrambled eggs, throw in a package of defrosted cooked shrimp and add soy sauce — lots of soy sauce. And I really have to run or I'll have burned rice for four!"

You have to second guess all the time. But be funny if they're looking for humor. Be brief and leave them wanting more — and wanting to see you again.

Be careful that your prepared monologue doesn't sound memorized. As an actor, you should have no trouble making it sound spontaneous. (Remember, they want real people types. If you sound memorized, you come off as an actor, not natural.) It really is a vicious circle. You have to be a good actor to fool them into thinking you're not acting.

Several years ago, I had been going on commercial auditions and not getting any. I wasn't getting any callbacks either. My agents kept sending me, so I knew I was an "in" type. At one audition, finally, the casting director screamed at me, "Iris, WHAT are you doing? Shakespeare? All you theater actors are the same. Give you a script and you turn into Lady MacBeth. Stop finishing your words. Most people don't. Stuff your mouth with hot potatoes and practice."

All the other casting directors simply thanked me, said "Very good," and send the next gal in. I was shocked. When they asked me to be natural, be myself, I never realized what good speech I always used. My enunciation was excellent. It was then I realized what they meant. They didn't want me. They wanted a very untheatrical, average person. Just like the ones selling their products on TV right now.

CHAPTER 10

TWENTY QUESTIONS

Another possibility, when there is no camera is what I call playing twenty questions. They literally ask you question after question.

1. Your name?
2. Your agent?
3. Where are you from?
4. Where did you go to school?
5. What sports are you good at?
6. Any kids . . . etc., etc.?

Now you can answer.

1. Iris Acker.
2. G.K. Management.
3. New York.
4. New York.
5. Swim, sail, snorkel.
6. Two.

Or you can make them remember you by answering in full interesting sentences.

1. My mother loved flowers, so she named me Iris, and I couldn't be happier about it.
2. I'm most fortunate to be represented by G.K. Management.

3.   I was born in New York, but I've lived in just
     about every state, as a result of traveling with
     plays and shows.
4.   We moved a lot when I was younger. I attended
     seven schools in fourteen years.
5.   I really must have been a fish in another life. I love
     to swim, snorkel and sail. I'm good at it, too.
6.   It's hard to think of my two boys as "kids." They
     tower over me and could lift me with one hand,
     although I feel very secure when my "children"
     are around.

See what I mean?

Even if you're told to go on camera and slate your name,
agent, height, size, hair and eye color, instead of:

"Iris Acker; G.K. Management; 5 feet 6; 10; strawberry
blond; blue."

Try: "Hi, there. I'm Iris Acker and I'm represented by G.K.
Management. I'm 5 feet 6 inches tall. I work very hard at
staying a size 10. My naturally curly hair is strawberry blond
and I have very blue eyes."

Prepare your own bio, in YOUR own words. Just be
interesting, but not cutesy.

CHAPTER 11

VOICE-OVERS

Auditioning for just the voice part of a TV or radio commercial is the same. Getting the voice-over audition is harder. If you have a unique voice, you will be remembered for it and called when they need your type of voice. If you are signed exclusively with one agent, he will send you on both voice-over and on-camera auditions.

A tape of your voice is your best calling card. If you think you're a good voice-over type, make a tape.

I didn't have a tape until I did about four radio spots. I asked for and received copies of the actual commercials. I took the individual tapes to a studio for editing (AFTRA gave me a list of several), and I added two more voice-overs from my television commercials reel. (I always ask for a copy of all my TV commercials. Sometimes I get them and sometimes not.) I choose very different and unique commercials, showing off my versatility.

Versatility is what I sell. If you have an announcer's voice, sell that. I do radio voice-overs on a regular basis for one particular voice-over producer who saw me (and heard me) in a play. I did three distinctly different characters in that play. I now do a variety of ten to twelve different characters for various radio commercials. (I mailed a tape to this producer a year before he saw my performance. He never listened to it until after he saw me in the play. Then, as a result of the play and the tape, he called me.)

Once you have the technique of working with a microphone, your theater experience will be your best asset.

The microphone, like a camera, must be your best friend. Someone you can talk to intimately. That does not mean getting too close to it. You will be told where to sit or stand for the best level. Again, as in a television audition, if they ask you for a level, start reading the copy. Be careful not to turn your head away from the microphone, or change your voice level once you start reading.

Watch your F's and T's, both at the beginning and the end of words. They'll say you're popping if you overdo your P's. Also, don't overpronounce R's and ER's at the ends of words.

If you can sing, you can use your vocal ability for several characters. Use your "head" voice for children and old ladies. Go to the bottom of the scale (vocalize down) for a sexy quality.

Theater actors can best "dress" for their audition. This time I don't mean in the actual clothes. My secret, or technique, is to visualize the wardrobe I'd be wearing if I were on stage. When I do old ladies, I prepare by pantomiming; putting on sensible oxford shoes, heavy stockings, thick eyeglasses and even a cane in my hand. (I can see it and feel it even though they can't.)

For a young girl, I visualize putting on pink socks, patent leather shoes (Mary Janes), a short ruffled dress and a big bow in my hair. I sit or stand pigeon-toed and knock-kneed. Yes, I get bewildered looks and dumfounded stares, but I also get the commercial, and you can, too.

On a television "on-camera" commercial audition, timing is not as important as it is on a radio audition. Practice reading commercials so you can finish in 30 seconds or 60 seconds, as needed. Tape some off the radio and try it. Tape yourself and compare.

Sometimes, you are given a script to be done in 30 seconds that you'll swear has 60 seconds of dialogue. Take a deep breath and do as much of the copy as possible in one breath. You'll save valuable time that way.

Persuading agents to send you on voice-over auditions is difficult even with a tape. Pursue it if you feel or have been told you're truly talented vocally. Call the agents in a different voice each time. If you have an answering machine, change the announcement often, using all your voices. Try to use a few on one announcement. Perhaps the snooty butler, then the "MAHSTER" talks, or grandpa puts his two cents in, etc.

At a voice-over audition, you can't dress in character, but do make a good impression by dressing as if you were applying for a sales position. Remember, your voice is auditioning from the first "hello" or "how do you do" on through the taping until you say good-bye.

Notes

CHAPTER 12

AGENTS, PICTURES
AND RESUMES

Your pictures are your first contact with an agent. The agent sees hundreds of them. Since the first step in getting to meet an agent is sending your picture, you can see how very important your pictures are. If you are handsome or beautiful, let your photo say so. Have the photographer take very flattering shots.

If your talent is your best asset, a good character composite is your best calling card.

As a beginner, I know you won't want to spend a lot of money, but if you don't have top notch pictures, you won't get an agent, or any auditions.

The best way to select a photographer is by looking at other actors' pictures. Ask who did them. Get names and numbers and call the photographers for prices. Make sure they will agree to re-do them if you're not happy with the first shooting.

When you get your "proofs," show them to several people. Get several opinions. Try to get an agent to look at them. Another actor's or a teacher's opinion can be helpful.

Be sure your photo looks like you. Don't have it retouched. Leave the lines. You're not fooling anyone. The agent will only ask how old the pictures are and suggest you have new ones taken.

Have at least one hundred photos made up at any of the special theatrical photo reproduction studios. An agent will want several and you'll be mailing out many.

Your resume should by typed and stapled to the back of your 8x10 glossy photo. Even if you have a composite or model card made, have an 8x10 glossy headshot as well. The composite says "model." The 8x10 glossy says "actor." If you have a lot of acting credits, your resume is no problem — as in this actor's:

JOHN STAR

Service: 431-1234	Height: 6 ft. 1 in.
Agent: 246-3579	Hair: Blond
	Eyes: Brown
	Suit: 40L

THEATRICAL EXPERIENCE

COMMERCIALS:	(Conflicts on Request)
BROADWAY:	*Henry and Harry in Indiana* .. Henry
	Sunrise Tomorrow .... Adam Brown
	The Teacher .... John Stone
OFF BROADWAY:	*Shakespeare's Revenge* ......Hamlet
	Horatio — Tic-Tac-Toe............. Myron Malone
	Aloysius .... The Widower
FILMS:	*Forever and Ever* .... Detective Coe
	Joe the Bartender .... Mr. Rogers
	Gotham's Glory ...... John Edwards
	Phil Fortune .... Dr. Phillips
INDUSTRIALS:	For: Breaker Boats
	Mop and Show
	Air Anywhere

SUMMER STOCK:	*Birdie's Bloopers* — Hal Winkle at The Vermont Monastery
	Heaven, Hell and You — Uncle Al at The Broken Barn (Maine)
SKILLS & SPORTS:	Swim, golf, ski, fish, drive a truck, dialects
TRAINING:	Columbia College for Drama
	Folger Film Academy

If you're just beginning, let's do it the following way: The heading is the same:

YOUR NAME

Your service number	Your height
Your agent	Your hair color
	Your eye color
	Suit or dress size

SPECIAL SKILLS:	Sing — voice range
	Dance — ballet or jazz
	Play guitar
	Dialects
	Any language other than English you speak fluently
	Type
SPORTS:	Tennis
	Golf
	Swim
	Snorkel
	Bowl
	Skate
TRAINING:	B.A. — Northwest University
	Drama
	Herbert Berghoff Actor's Studio
	Commercial training with Iris Acker

What you're doing is taking up space with things you *CAN* do. If you haven't done any commercials, you simply say you have nothing running when you are asked.

Please put down *YOUR* special skills, and *YOUR* sports, and *YOUR* training. Listing it one under the other takes up space.

I use several resumes. They all say the same thing, but I rotate the order on the page. If I'm going on a film audition, I use my resume with the film credits listed first.

FILMS   ....
                         ....
                         ....
THEATER   ....
                         ....
                         ....
SKILLS   ....
                         ....
                         ....

If I'm going on a theater audition, I use my resume with my theater credits listed first.

THEATER   ....
                         ....
                         ....
FILMS   ....
                         ....
                         ....
TELEVISION   ....
                         ....
                         ....
SKILLS   ....
                         ....
                         ....

The person for whom you are auditioning will assume you value your film experience (or theater, according to which audition) most. It's only good psychology to have them think you consider yourself a film (or theater) actor above all. Certainly, if it's a commercial audition, that will lead the list.

Now we're ready to meet the agents. The accepted procedure is to mail a picture and resume and follow through with a phone call about a week later requesting an interview.

Or, you might phone several agents and ask their procedures for meeting new talent. Another actor can help you. If you are lucky enough to have a friend who will introduce you personally to his agent, that will help. Any personal recommendation will help.

It can also hurt. My friend, Doreen Stenzel, a very successful commercial actress, was called back on a mop commercial. The agent told her she was definite for the "after" portion of the commercial, meaning she was the woman who used the sponsor's mop and looked neat and lovely while mopping the house. They were looking for a "before" woman, a good character actress with a very expressive face who plays "messy" well. Doreen immediately thought of me. (No, my ego was not hurt.) She encouraged the agent to send me on the audition. He found my picture in his files and agreed.

I not only got the commercial, but Doreen was eliminated. It was decided I could be both the before and after; that I was so versatile, able to look super messy and super great, and carry through with the reading for both segments, that they could save a salary by using just me.

Never was I so embarrassed, so unhappy to get a job. Only because Doreen and I were such good friends and the fact that she got another commercial (a better paying one) for the same day was I saved.

I worked a lot through the agent who sent me on that commercial after that, and I've been trying to pay Doreen back for her help ever since.

Any excuse to stay in touch or contact an agent is

good. A showcase appearance. Even if they don't come, send a flyer with your name on it before the show. A program mailed after.

Have postcards made with your picture on them and mail once a month. Send Valentine's Day cards, Halloween cards, Christmas in July cards, anything that will keep your name in front of them or make them remember you.

If you're ever going to give an agent a gift, give something for his desk. A letter opener, a paper clip box, a stapler. Something that will make him think of you every day.

Many agents have "open hours." Find out when and "make rounds." Have a picture postcard in your hand and leave it.

Try to adopt a signature gimmick of yourself to leave. I'm easy because my name is Iris. Not only is it still a unique name, it's also a flower. I have wooed agents of my choice with one long-stemmed Iris every time I visited their office. How about distinctive stationary you can jot a note on? So distinctive that after several visits or mailings you won't even have to sign it.

Can you write poetry? Jingles? Make your notes rhyme. Use green or purple ink!

I'm sure you will think of many more ideas.

When you are finally sent on an audition, a thank you card and an "Any casting today?" note will help. Persevere and prepare for lots of rejection. (A callback is almost as good as getting the commercial. You'll know you read well and were physically right.)

When you are interviewed by an agent, *SPARKLE*. Be enthusiastic. My favorite agent was in an absolute "funk" the day we first met. It was raining. Business was bad. He had a headache. Everything was against me, but . . . I wore a bright green raincoat (I always wear bright colors on a rainy day) which he immediately commented on. It didn't help his headache, but it made him smile. He told me business was very slow. I told him that was today, but I had it from a very good source that good times were coming, and now that we had finally met, I was sure of it!

I bubbled, I effervesced, and I definitely changed his mood by the time I left. He sent me on an audition the next day. An audition where he could only send *ONE* actor for each role. I had really sold him. You can, too.

Try to meet the casting directors at advertising agencies. "Ross Report," in New York, lists their policies (available at AFTRA or at their offices at 40-29 27th Street, Long Island City, NY 11101). Although the advertising agencies seldom call talent directly, they do request specific actors through the agents. And when you meet new agents, be sure to tell them which casting directors you know.

Make sure you have an answering service or an answering machine, unless there is always someone home to take messages. You never want to miss a call. They won't call back again and again.

I hope *YOUR* next call for your next audition will get you "that commercial" and that this book helped.

CHAPTER 13

REJECTION

Now that we've finally decided to go out there and audition for commercials, after preparing ourselves with the proper photographs and resumes, and also with the knowledge and techniques necessary, are we prepared to accept the constant rejection?

Rejection, according to the Merriam Webster Dictionary, is:

1. To refuse to acknowledge or submit to;
2. To refuse to take or accept;
3. To refuse to grant, consider or accede to;
4. To throw back or out, as useless or unsatisfactory.

Since this is a "how to" book, I offer this advice. Accept the fact that your turn will come. It's a matter of percentages. If twenty-five actors audition for one commercial, your chances obviously are one in twenty-five of getting it. Yet, I've seen actors suffer from the rejection of not being the lucky one, as if they personally were singled out to suffer for all the twenty-four actors not chosen as well.

If an agent sends you out to audition for commercials, you are a good commercial type.

If you get called back, even only occasionally, you must be doing something right. Hang in there. Be patient. It takes lots of auditions to land one commercial.

Equip yourself with all the proper tools:

Good pictures,

A good resume,

A good "commercial" education (This book and perhaps a good commercial class),

Sturdy walking shoes for making rounds,

AND

A healthy, positive, knowledgeable attitude regarding rejection.

When I check to see if I've been cast in a commercial I've auditioned for and am told they are not using me, I shrug my shoulders and say, "Their loss, I'll get the next one." And if I don't get the next one, or the one after that, I know *ONE* is coming up with my name on it. Yes, some of us get more than others, but that may be only because our type is more in demand. If rejection is going to present a serious problem for you, don't waste your time trying.

I took Michael Shurtleff's "How to Audition for Theater" class in New York. The thing he said that I've never forgotten was:

"If there's anything you enjoy doing other than acting — painting, sewing, plumbing, etc. — please do it. But if you think you'll *DIE* if you can't be an actor, welcome to my class."

That's a little strong for commercial acting, but if you're going to die a little each time you are rejected, please, find another way to earn money.

I like to think I'm not auditioning for *THAT* specific commercial, but it's more like a general audition. If they don't use me for *THIS* commercial because I'm not right for it, six months from now, when I am right, they'll request me and book me.

This actually happened to me. I auditioned for a vacuum

cleaner commercial. Everyone I knew was "called back" except me. Six months later I auditioned for a gas and electric company and got booked.

On the set, I asked the client, "Why me, for this spot?" He said I made them laugh again. He reminded me of the vacuum commercial, for which I was physically wrong. They liked my reading so much though, they were determined to use me eventually and they did.

Not only do you have to cope with constant rejection, you have to deal with exasperation. A not untypical day for me recently began with a bus ride to my first audition. Only after I got off the bus did I realize I had left my portfolio of pictures at home. Not to be late, I chose to proceed without it.

I went to the wrong address. The casting director had moved. The agent had neglected to tell me. I taxied to the correct address and arrived huffing and puffing.

My next call was across town. Detouring for my pictures, I arrived *JUST* in time amid a few snickers. It seems I was the wrong color! "Which agent sent you and why is he punishing you?" the casting director asked.

Too early for my next audition (back on the other side of town), I had lunch, window shopped and generally killed time. When I finally showed up my usual half-hour early, the receptionist greeted me with, "Where were you? You're two hours late. The casting is over. We had to send one of the other actresses in twice to be a wife with your 'husband' in the commercial."

I don't think I ever convinced them that the agent gave me the wrong time, and I was killing time in the neighborhood, not to be too early.

Three different agents were involved. If I was just starting out in this business, that day may very well have been my last day. Instead, I called my manager and cried to him, then called my very good friend, Gloria Gonzalez, and recounted my day with such humor it inspired her to write a play.

The moral of all this is that I chose to include these three exasperating auditions in with the percentages, again shrugging and thinking, "Their loss, the next one will be mine."

CHAPTER 14

AN ACTUAL DAY OF SHOOTING

ON LOCATION:

Congratulations, you got your first commercial and you're told you are going on location to shoot. On location is anywhere other than a TV studio: a bank, a store, a park, an airport, etc.

You can expect to be told to either meet a bus or a limousine at a convenient location (near the advertising agency, the production company, a bus terminal), or you'll be told to proceed to the location site.

Certainly, be prompt and early. You'll be asked to bring wardrobe if it's a contemporary shoot with clothes you may own. The wardrobe person will probably call you the day before to discuss possible outfits. (You are paid for wearing your own clothes.)

You may be asked instead to attend a wardrobe "call," either with your clothes for them to approve, or to be fitted with clothes they have bought or are making for you.

On location, the way to appear most professional is to keep your mouth shut. Don't ask questions. Wait to be told what to do. Of course, there will be lots said and done you've never seen or heard before. Write down all the new words and actions, and the next day, call an experienced actor or technician friend to define and explain what you heard or saw. Don't gamble on showing your inexperience and nervousness by saying the wrong things.

Arrive with a clean face, minus makeup. Usually, makeup is applied as soon as you arrive (after coffee and doughnuts). Hopefully, if there is a script, you've had it for several days and memorized it. Hopefully, they haven't rewritten or changed it. If they have, that's the next thing discussed. Meanwhile, lights are being set. Sound is being tested. A small body mike may be taped to you or placed on you with a trailing wire. The sound man will take levels. (You'll be expected to say the actual script.)

Wardrobe is next. Once you're made up and in wardrobe, they'll place you on the set, in the lights, for testing.

Then you will rehearse. Listen to the director. Be aware of the camera. Sometimes, you don't get to work for hours. Another segment might shoot fist, or there are problems with lights, the camera or the set. Relax and stay on the set. Don't disappear, stay and watch.

The set will be filled with people. In addition to the technicians (for lights, sound, camera, makeup and wardrobe), there will be people representing the advertising agency and the production company, including an assistant director, a script girl, gaffer and grips (the men who push the cameras, lights and set around), and the client, or someone representing the client, will be there.

Now the fun begins. Everyone has another idea how the script should be read, or the product shown, or what you should wear, etc., etc., etc. You have to please everyone. Meaning, be prepared to do it many different ways. The director's way, the advertising agency's way, and the client's way as well. Many "takes" are done and only when the commercial is finally edited is it decided which "take" they will use.

Be prepared, before each take, for a technician to put a

small blackboard (the slate) in front of you and say the name of the product and "take one" or "take two" and so on. The slate will have the product name, the director's name, and which "take" they are doing (1, 2 or 101) written on it. He will clap the boards supporting the slate and the director will say, "Ready," or "Stand By," and "Action," and YOU speak or move or follow the actual direction.

If you goof, apologize (simply say "sorry" and they will redo it). They'll goof, too (problems with lights, sound or the camera). They will stop to reload the camera with film.

Many times it's a tape commercial, and they can do an instant replay on a TV monitor. You should look at it, too, so you can correct any problems.

When you break for lunch, don't rush to the buffet table, because the crew eats first (their union's rule). When you are done for the day, offer to buy a copy of the commercial and a couple of "still" prints, if there was a "still" photographer shooting. Ask the assistant director who you should contact, and in a few weeks, follow through. If you are lucky, they will give you a copy of the commercial, gratis, and a few prints, too.

You may be asked to hang around after the shooting to do some "wild tracking." You'll simply be asked to repeat your dialogue, to be recorded without filming. You may be asked to do a specific line many different ways.

"It's a wrap," signals the end of the day. Say a personal good-bye to the client, advertising men and director, and be sure to thank the crew.

If your commercial is to be shot in a studio, you'll go directly there, and otherwise the situation is the same as on location.

CHAPTER 15

POINTS OF VIEW FROM OTHERS

Casting Director — Lori S. Wyman

Talent Agent — Tammy J. Green

Makeup Artist — Chere

Commercial Director — Joe Adler

Photographer — Bob Lasky —
The Perfect Picture

Commercial Actress — Judy Upton

CASTING DIRECTOR — LORI S. WYMAN

When I was asked to write my views as a Casting Director and what I felt was important for an actor to make it in this business, I knew it had to be the most important factor in an actor's career.

As I have been casting over the past twelve years, I have seen many mistakes which have cost an actor his part. The one thing, however, is that they all stem from the same root.

Attitude is, in my estimation, the most important trait an actor can display. There's a good attitude, bad attitude, indifference, anger, self-pity — I've seen them all. If the actor doesn't display a positive attitude, he is very hard to work with. It's very difficult to deal with an actor who knows it all or one who facially editorializes every time they finish an audition.

One of my pleasures in casting is helping the actor with their audition. When an actor comes in and knows everything, then my job is over before it starts. Or maybe I thought the audition was good and the actor facially tells me how bad it was before I even had a chance to evaluate it myself. Let the Casting Directors give as much input as they choose before you sway their thinking in a negative way.

If you walk into a casting with the attitude that you are not going to get the part, chances are excellent that you won't. Don't let the competition across the room determine how you feel about your own performance.

When you walk into the casting and hand your picture to the Casting Director, don't start making excuses for it. I can't begin to explain how often an actor has handed his headshot and resume to me and then proceeded to tell me that the headshot doesn't really look like him anymore and that his resume isn't up-to-date. Then why are you giving it to me? Don't you want a job from me? Why would you hand me your materials and then proceed to invalidate it? Yet, I can't tell you how many times I get this in a single casting. Don't defeat yourself before you've begun. If you feel insecure about the materials you are presenting, then update them right away. Why would I want to hire someone who doesn't believe in themselves?

I understand that an actor gets nervous when they come into an audition, but don't let it affect you in a negative way. You see, your attitude determines whether you make it or break it at an audition. Have fun at a casting, be positive when you walk in, if you get the job then it's a bonus. A *POSITIVE ATTITUDE* will get you places in this business, and in life.

. . . .

Ms. Wyman received her degree in Speech/Communications from the University of Miami. Her television credits include four seasons of *Miami Vice*, a season of *B. L. Stryker*, *Wiseguy*, and episodes of *21 Jump Street*. Her film credits include *Running Scared*, *Revenge of the Nerds* and *Blind Fury*. She is currently a member of Women of the Motion Picture Industry, and the Florida Motion Picture & Television Association.

TALENT AGENT — TAMMY GREEN

One of the most difficult aspects of an acting career is getting started. As Agency Director of the Green and Green Agency, I can attest that our phones oftentimes ring with anxious beginners seeking advice. Just as an accountant needs a reliable adding machine and a carpenter needs his hammer and nails, the actor must also be equipped with the right tools.

An introductory commercial acting class with an overview of both the audition process and agent representation is invaluable. We expect that the actors we represent know the basics of how to introduce themselves to potential clients. This includes a friendly, clean and confident appearance, the correct wardrobe, and most importantly, the ability to listen to instructions given by the agent, and then the client or Casting Director. The agent can get you to the audition, and then the actor must sell himself. A self-knowledge of *WHAT MAKES YOU, THE ACTOR, THE ONLY CHOICE FOR THE JOB* is essential!

We also insist that the actors who are represented by Green and Green have headshots and resumes. Even a beginner should invest in an 8x10 that will augment the live audition. Most clients refer to the headshot and resume to see that the actor has some experience or at least a professional presentation. For beginners, we suggest that they list schooling, skills and goals.

It is the agent's objective to see that the actor is being seen and being hired. A successful agent/actor relationship will allow for constructive advice and periodic success assessment. When an agent takes the time to explain to a performer how they can improve, it is a time to take note rather than take offense.

Remember, the acting profession is a difficult and uncertain career to choose. Professionalism and preparation on the part of both the agent and "the actor" will make the difficult paths a bit easier.

. . . .

Tammy J. Green and sister/partner Lauren Green are the Agency Directors of Green and Green Model and Talent Agency with offices located in Miami and Chicago. They have represented actors in national and international ad campaigns, television series and major motion pictures.

MAKEUP ARTIST — CHERE

How to Make Up for Commercial Auditions

Looking your best is very important. Makeup, hair and clothes must reflect a sense of the part you're auditioning for.

To start, here are some supplies you'll need:

Moisturizers	Eyeshadows	Lipsticks (pink, mauve,
Bases	Eyeliner pencils	coral, red)
Concealers	Eyebrow pencils	Brow brushes
Blushes	Mascaras	Colorless gloss

Most actors and models, male and female, need to look at the pouches or circles under the eyes. True "bags" can result from a weakening of skin tone, loss of elasticity, or from too much or too little sleep, or from a sinus condition. Whatever the reason, here are some suggestions for camouflaging.

Apply your foundation first. Use a base half a tone *DARKER* than your normal shade. Apply a lighter concealer to the shadowed area under the eyes only.

If you have *DEEP* circles, use a base half a tone *LIGHTER* and use the concealer, too. If your casting is for a mother, teacher or "girl next door" look, keep your makeup natural and "low-key." Not too much blush and not too hot of a lip color.

Your hair can be pulled back in a "ponytail" or in a "bouncy" loose style. Don't tease or over spray.

If your casting is for someone older, darken the circles under your eyes and alongside your nasal labial fold.

If it's in fashion, make up your eyes. Blend two or three shades of shadow, very well. Apply liner *UNDER* your eyes. Use stronger blush. Outline your lips with liner and wear lipstick to match your outfit.

Fortunately, a makeup artist/hair stylist is almost always on the set, so . . . Good luck, there's lots of work out there.

. . . .

As a makeup artist, Chere's credits include the television shows *Hollywood Squares*, *Big Break*, and *Attitudes*. In theater, she has done *Barnum* and *Ain't Misbehavin'*, and in commercials and print, she has done work for all the leading department stores and numerous fashion products. Celebrities she has worked on include such notables as Natalie Cole, Phyllis Diller, Estelle Getty, Robin Leach, Robert Culp, Gloria Estefan, Susan Rattan, Isabella Rossellini, and Nancy Stafford.

Karen Montero — A sophisticated look.
Photography by Lasky.

Karen Montero — A casual look.
Photography by Lasky.

COMMERICAL DIRECTOR — JOE ADLER

To me, the audition should start the minute the actor gets the phone call from the agent. Then, the attitude, the approach and state of mind, while getting to the audition, is very important. Arrive early, and concentrate. I'm turned off by actors wasting valuable time socializing.

I have a Casting Director put the talent on tape; then I prefer to watch the tape alone. For out-of-town clients, we send them a duplicate tape, then confer for callbacks on the phone. It's really a joint effort; a combination of minds, between the art director, the copy writer, the account people and myself. I always fight for the people I want, but sometimes your second choice wins after a consensus.

I do look for actors who project an open, optimistic, energetic presence, with dead-on eye contact to the camera. It's dangerous to get too cutesy when you "slate" or introduce yourself. Nor should you be overbearing.

We're buying a quality. Learn to be confident. That's where classes help. Leave the actor home. Just bring yourself to that lens. Take the time to analyze the script. Read between the lines. What are they trying to project with you? What do they really want you to portray?

On the set: The first four hours you sit and wait, after makeup and wardrobe, then you do endless takes. Learn how to use your "down" time effectively. Learn not to waste energy. It's all about relaxation and concentration, and you must not squander performance.

Now, you must learn there's a tremendous amount of insecurity in the people behind the camera. If you see them consulting between takes, don't take that as rejection of your performance and blow your concentration. Ninety percent of the time they're not talking about you. Thirty or forty takes is not unusual. Keep up your pacing and your energy.

I believe in "indirection" more than direction. Sometimes, the client will criticize an actor's performance and suggest direction. I'll go to the actor and say "They love you; it's going beautifully," and his next two takes are dynamite, and the client thinks it's his "misdirection" which did it.

I always tell actors, it doesn't pay to get depressed if you don't get it. Take your best shot and take the attitude, "They're wrong, it's their mistake and their loss."

. . . .

Joe Adler studied drama at Carnegie Mellon in Pittsburgh, PA, and film at The New York University School of Film.

He has won numerous "Addy" Awards and a "Clio" for Best Humor Award.

He has won the South East Writers Association "Carbonnel" Award for Best Direction of a Play two times.

He has directed hundreds of commercials and four feature films. He directed a two-hour cable movie, *Doubles* (from the play of the same name), which will serve as a "pilot" for the series.

PHOTOGRAPHER — BOB LASKY

The Perfect Picture

What is the perfect picture? In short, the perfect picture is the picture that gets you in the door, so you can show the client or Casting Director "your stuff."

To start in commercials, in most cases, all one needs is a good smiling headshot. If you do not show your teeth, they will take it for granted that you have none. Unless you are a character actor, an energetic headshot will do the trick.

Show the client that you are comfortable in front of the camera; therefore, choose your photographer carefully.

1. Find and Interview the Photographer.
    a. A good way to find a photographer is by looking at photo credits of other talent's headshots.
    b. See samples of the photographer's work. Make sure that the photographer is a commercial headshot photographer.
    c. Discuss fees (know what is included for that fee). Sometimes, going the cheap route for your head-shot can cost you jobs that would more than make up for the difference in rates.
    d. Have confidence that the photographer can capture your personality on film. Feel comfortable with the photographer or do not shoot with him/her.
2. What to Wear
    a. Simple collar lines (polo, button-down collar, denim shirts, crewneck sweaters).
    b. Solid, middle-tone colors work best. You are selling you, not the shirt.
    c. Women, if your ears are pierced, wear stud earrings only. Men, leave your earring home for this one. No necklaces for men or women.

   d. No turtlenecks for commercial headshots. If you
      cover your neck, they will think that you have a scar,
      mole or hickey.
      NOTE: Bring at least six shirts to choose from.
3. The Shoot
   a. Be well rested. Get plenty of sleep the night before
      your shoot.
   b. Have your picture taken the time of day that your
      eyes look the best (late morning is the best time for
      most people).
   c. Have fun! Sure you're nervous, but you're working
      with a pro, and at worst, if the session does not
      come out well, a reputable photographer will give
      you a reshoot.
   d. SMILE, ENERGY, CONFIDENCE,
      YOU — YOU — YOU! ! !

Now you have your contact sheets; these are the 8x10
sheets with 36 small pictures that you will need an 8x10 loop
to see. Most camera stores carry them; if a loop is not attain-
able, a strong magnifying glass will do.

Take your contacts home and study them. Show them to
other people in the business. Go over them with your photographer. I usually check off some good ones to help new talent
see themselves properly for this field. If you already have an
agent or coach and they have time, go over the contacts
with them.

Go for energy, not just a nice picture. You must look right
back at the person looking at the picture. That picture must
say something, because in many cases (picture pulls) your
picture will be all that the client has to go on.

If you also wish to do print, you will need to have a composite card made. That is usually a 6x8 card with two to five
pictures on it. Clients, especially for print, will need to see you
from your neck down, in different outfits and situations.

Before you spend your hard-earned money, have a very good idea of where you fit in. Fashion, Beauty, Lifestyle or Character model are four of the major categories.

Discuss your look with your photographer, agent or coach; but again, make sure that you are dealing with people who have a grip on the business. Do not bring in a bunch of clothes and haphazardly shoot meaningless pictures. *PLAN!!*

Whatever you do, do not try to fit the square peg into the round hole. Look in the mirror, know your positive and negative points. Know any height restrictions for modeling in your area. Be realistic about your weight. Look at your face realistically (eyes, nose, mouth, complexion) for beauty modeling. Look at your magazine ads and TV commercials and see where you fit in. One of the keys to success in this field is to know your space and go for it!

Be happy with who you are, it will show through on your pictures and in your castings.

. . . .

Bob Lasky has worked extensively with advertising agencies in both America and Europe. Most of his work deals in fashion, glamour, beauty and celebrity photography, as well as music photography (album covers, concerts, promo, etc.).

His work has appeared in *Vogue, People, Teen, Mademoiselle, Cosmopolitan, Harper's Bazaar, Seventeen, TV Guide, Billboard, Rolling Stone, Metro Magazine, Headliner,* as well as many other publications.

A partial list of his musical clients include: Elvis Presley, Frank Sinatra, The Bee Gees, Jimmy Cliff, Miami Sound Machine, Benny Goodman, Chuck Mangione, and Stanley Turrentine.

Bob has also photographed various Miss America, Miss

USA, Miss Florida and other pageant winners, and has been called upon on numerous occasions to judge many prestigious beauty pageants.

COMMERICAL ACTRESS — JUDY UPTON

Success as an actor in the television commercial business is more than a smile and handshake. It takes training, hard work, dedication and a stiff upper lip.

Acting in commercials requires a special technique. Even if you have trained for the theater or film, you may not be prepared for television commercial acting. You've taken a wise first step by committing yourself to this book. Take legitimate classes. Learn the technique the right way. You'll save time getting started and enhance your reputation quickly.

That's how I started. I carried a copy of the first edition of this manual in my car to every audition and referred to the appropriate chapter while preparing for every audition. Now, barely five years later, I've done more than 70 national, regional, local and foreign commercials. I learned the basic fundamentals from Iris and other professionals. My career has now expanded into other areas: industrial films, television and video voice-overs, TV, film, theater, and print work as a lifestyle and character model and actress. I even do body parts. Because talent agencies that handle commercial talent often handle other aspects of the business, you can expand your business, and you don't have to be in New York or Los Angeles to have a busy and successful career.

I believe I stay successful by maintaining chameleon-like flexibility with a variety of looks; sometimes my own parents don't recognize me! It's important not to stereotype yourself — or let others. I did establish myself at first as an All-American Mom (there are a lot of parent parts) to etch Judy Upton in the right minds, but QUICKLY followed up with an array of personas to convince them they couldn't dare forget this talent.

Of course, I trained in commercial technique. I can walk

and talk and have a good commercial look which is real but somewhat calculated. I watch TV commercials religiously for style, wardrobe, makeup, hair, character types, ad campaigns, any detail. Just take a quick look at a few of the choices of headshots and composites I can present at auditions. I have everything from upscale glamorous to All-American anyone, to business/spokesperson, lifestyle/real person to my "Kookie Kamp" of characters (the latter, all Addy Award winners). My hair length is cut so that not only can it be styled straight, but curled or swept up. With my hair color, I could have a blonde or brunette family or spokespartner. Because I film for Latin America as well, I'm prepared for that, too. I rinse my hair darker on request.

I have a gap in my front teeth that I chose not to have bonded, a helpful option when necessary. Instead, I have an excellent quality insert. So, I even have flexibility with my teeth. I use the gap for characters and "real" people; the insert is used for upscale business and yuppie characters. Sometimes, I even give the client the choice. I also have a collection of character and period clothing from which to choose for auditions and shoots. And, you should see the eyeglasses I've collected.

Don't stereotype yourself — or let others. You can analyze yourself, too. Just watch TV. See who the advertisers are buying now. Have fun. Be creative. Be open. This business is just that, a business. And hard work, too.

Don't be depressed if you don't get a commercial. There is always another one. Don't denigrate yourself, your experience, your ability, your looks. You only hurt yourself. You need your positive attitude. You were seen. You added to your audition experience. You may just not have been the type the director/client was looking for. Don't zigzag. Be true to yourself. Be your basic self.

If you start trying to second guess the client, you'll go crazy. You'll end up zigging when you should have zagged and develop a bad case of the "if's." Self-confidence is a very important factor in booking a commercial. Work hard to maintain it.

My biggest complaint is not getting enough information about the audition so that I can prepare character, wardrobe, style. I ask questions. You must get answers from your agent (don't expect to get straight answers, but try). Be clear about your audition before you enter the auditioning studio. Your work reflects on you.

The most important factor of all is eye contact. Whether you are meeting an agent, the Casting Director, the client and director on your callback, and especially when relating to the camera, maintain eye contact. The importance of any expression is in the eyes; your inner energy as well as animation.

To stay successful, don't forget the basics; have a positive attitude and Eye Contact!

> Be prepared.
> Be punctual and reliable.
> Be real and natural.
> Show personality and range.
> Show confidence.
> Don't judge yourself.
> Listen.
> Eliminate surprises.
> Be flexible and creative.
> Have a variety of looks.
> Treat this effort as the business it is.

As a beginner, or an established actor, don't let up. Bring constant attention to yourself and your work. Don't become complacent. There is always someone new coming along, eager and hungry.

Hang In There . . . Have Fun!

See you on TV and Break a Leg.

. . . .

COMPOSITE SHEETS

Photography by Lasky.

Commercial actress — Judy Upton.
Photography by Lasky.

Commercial actress — Judy Upton.
Photography by Lasky.

As opposed to a bio for Ms. Upton, here is her resume. It's a real good format for you to follow!

JUDY UPTON
SAG/AFTRA

HAIR: Dark Blonde
EYES: Brown

HEIGHT: 5'4"
WEIGHT: 105

COMMERCIALS: (Conflicts on Request) over 70 national, regional, local & foreign
VOICE-OVERS: (Conflicts on Request) Demo Cassettes & Reels available
Spokesperson, Character Voices, Dubbing, 'Toons, Technical & Medical Jargon (M.S. BioMedical Sciences)

INDUSTRIALS:

General Foods Beverage Div.	Field Reporter Vicki Gordon
Nestle's	Sales Representative
Lever Brothers	Sales Representative
Kraft Dairy Products	Spokesperson
American Hospital Supply Corp.	Spokesperson
Ryder Moving Services	Housewife, Mover, Truck Driver
Digital Equipment Corp.	Flapper, Prom Queen, Bobbysoxer
Personnel Pool of America	Spokesperson, Personnel Coordinator
Medical Personnel Pool of America	Spokesperson, Staff Coordinator
Amerada Hess Co. (3) (Animatics)	Station Attendant, Housewife
American Bankers Ins. Group	Business Manager Joan Sandler
Blockbuster Video Stores (Animatics)	Wife & Mother
Pantry Pride	Bakery Lady
Pier 66 Hotel Resort & Marina	Guest and Wife
Jaffe's Office Products	Businessperson & Customer
Miami-Dade Community College	Spokesperson

TELEVISION:

Miami Vice (Universal — NBC)	Organized Crime Bureau Secretary
The Jury Box (PBS)	The Jury Foreman
Tee Talk (PBS)	Golf Show Demonstrator
Ye Olde World Furniture Faire (WLRN) Live	Presenter (twice)
Women's View (WLRN — Miami)	Miami Dolphin's NFL Logo Products
Loves of Your Life (Music Video)	The Bride

FEATURE FILM:
Making Mr. Right (Orion Pictures): Directed by Susan Seidelman; with John Malkovich
Scientist; Stand-in for lead, Frankie; Photo double for Frankie's sister, Ivy

THEATER:

Onstage, *A Night Uptown — Hooray for Hollywood*	"A Chorus Line" Lead Chorine
FMPTA Press Forum (Live)	Wife in commercial spoof
Valentine's Day Murder Mystery	Virginia A. Madden (Suspect)

Bridgeton (NJ) Community Players:
Annie Get Your Gun: Jessie, Annie's impish sister
Brigadoon: Jean MacLeron, second lead, innocent romantic bride-to-be
Alice Mulford's Little Theater (NJ): Wide variety of roles

TRAINING:

Ray Forchion (L.A.) Workshop/Seminar
"Acting for Film and Television" Workshops with Jeremiah Comey (L.A.)
The Tony Shepherd Seminar (Casting Director for Aaron Spelling Productions)
   "Acting for Television Workshop"
David Man Seminar — Workshop (New York) // The AFTRA Actors' Workshops
The Michael Stark Workshops // Beverly McDermott's Film & TV Acting Seminar
Robbie Buckley Burns Dramatic Arts Center (Improv & Soap Opera Technique)
Connie Zimet's Commercial Copy Workshop & Advanced Voice-over Workshop
Commercial Training Workshop with Iris Y. Acker (Improv and Script)
Advanced Commercial Training with Iris Y. Acker (Those Who Cast)
Film Training with Iris Y. Acker
M.S.: Seton Hall University   B.A.: Catawba College (Biology)

SPORTS

Tennis   Golf   Swimming   Jogging   Snorkeling   Jet Ski
   Cert. SCUBA   Bicycling   Softball/Baseball   Bowling   Aerobics

SPECIAL SKILLS & ASSETS

TelePrompter-proficient, Laboratory Skills, Cashier, Excellent Hands & Feet,
Natural Nails

MEMBERSHIPS

Women of the Motion Picture Industry (S. Florida Chapter, Treasurer and Exec.
Board Member) Florida Motion Pictures & Television Association (Greater Ft. Laud-
erdale Chapter) Professional Actors' Association of Florida (PAAF)

EPILOGUE

Although you will be spending money on pictures and postage, if you can afford it, take classes. Not only classes in "commercials," which can be expensive in New York and California (although very worthwhile), but in improvisation, scene study or mime.

Shop around, make calls, ask other actors. A class is the best place to meet other actors and make friends. Go to any audition that gives you the opportunity to read or perform. Generally, that seems to be a non-union theater or film audition, where no agent is involved. It's important that you have the opportunity to fail in front of a group of strangers — the opportunity to be nervous and to make mistakes. Only in a class or at an audition can you test your talent.

So go out there, make a fool of yourself, pick yourself up, and start all over again!

DEFINITIONS

Action: Start talking or movement according to direction.

Booking: You have been hired for the job. It is most unprofessional to cancel a booking for any reason!!

Callback: The client has narrowed down his choices and would like to see you again at a specific time. Please wear the same wardrobe.

Call time: The time you are to arrive on the set. Please be 15 minutes early.

Casting/Audition: A specific appointment, set up with a client for a specific job.

Clap stick: Sticks used before each shot to synchronize sound with picture.

Composite: Several photographs on a designed card with statistics, to be used by you and the agency. You must have a composite for print work, fashion or lifestyle.

C.U.: Close up.

Cut: Stop action.

D.V.: Direct voice — on camera.

Dissolve: Action fades out of one scene into another.

Dubbing, to dub: Match your words against the action or lip movement of the picture.

E.C.U.: Extreme close-up.

First refusal: The client would like you to keep specific dates available. They have not booked you nor are they responsible to pay you at this time. If another job conflicts with the "first refusal dates," *LET THEM KNOW IMMEDIATELY! ! ! ! !*

Gaffer: Head electrician.

Go see/interview: An appointment, set by the agency to see you in general.

Grips: Stage hands who grip things.

Headshot: A photograph of your head with your name on it. They should have a flat finish, and you should have several on file at an agency. Check often to see that they have enough headshots.

It's a wrap: The commercial is finished shooting.

Location: Where the commercial will be shot other than a studio.

M.C.U.: Medium close-up.

On bells: Silence on the set. Sound is recording.

Pan (right or left): Camera is directed to follow the action to the right or left.

Print it: A good take, for possible use.

Props: Any item used in the shot.

A shot: A piece of action recorded by the camera.

Slate: The board which is photographed at the beginning of each scene for every take, with scene and take numbers on it.

Speed: Spoken by the sound man, to indicate film and tape ready for recording.

Strike it: Remove it.

Storyboard: A series of sketches in boxes, to guide the talent, the director, the script girl, etc.

Take: One scene which has been photographed.

Talent: The actors.

Voice-over: An off-screen voice (or narrator).

Voucher: An agreement with you and the client that mentions specific terms. Give a signed copy to the client, keep one for your files and mail the remaining copy to the agent within 48 hours of your job.

Weather day: Keep this additional day open in case of rain or other weather conditions that would prohibit shooting. It is the responsibility of the producers to cancel you if a weather day occurs, so . . . unless you are told otherwise, show up!

An agent: A person who is called by either a casting director, a production house, or an advertising agency to get actors for an audition.

A casting director: Someone who casts commercials for an advertising agency, a film company or a production house. He either works directly for them or is in business for himself and is called by them to cast the commercial. He then calls the agents to send actors to him to audition.

A manager: Should be:

1. An advisor on all levels, working toward building the actor's career.
2. A middleman between agent and client.
3. A mother.
4. A father.
5. A "shrink."

TALENT UNIONS

A.E.A.	Actor's Equity Association
A.F.M.	American Federation of Musicians
A.F.T.R.A.	American Federation of Television and Radio Artists
A.G.M.A.	American Guild of Musical Artists
A.G.V.A.	American Guild of Variety Artists
S.A.G.	Screen Actor's Guild

You can go on any S.A.G. or A.F.T.R.A. commercial audition as a *PRINCIPAL* without being a member. In New York and California, you must be a member of S.A.G. or A.F.T.R.A. to be an "extra" in either of these union's commercials.

A complete listing of all the S.A.G. and A.F.T.R.A. agents can be obtained at any of their local agencies.

COMMERCIAL CHECK LIST

When you get to see yourself on a TV monitor, check yourself on these items:

Do I overdo?
Have I got eye contact?
Am I relating to the camera (intimately)?
Am I holding the copy so that I only have to lower my eyes to read?
Have I mastered how to read a cue card?
Have I remembered to memorize the first and last line?
Have I remembered the "tag?"
Am I pronouncing the product correctly?
Am I bobbing my head?
Am I talking with my hands?
How do I look in the color I've chosen?
Does my hair style flatter me?
Am I believable?

Notes

PERFORMER'S BAG

This will be your working wardrobe and should be kept clean and pressed at all times.

MEN: Khaki trousers
Navy blazer
2 Lacoste or Izod type shirts in solid colors
2 man-tailored shirts with button-down collars in pastel colors
1 dress shirt in a pastel color
1 tie with foulard pattern (prefer red with small pattern)
1 pair of loafers in brown or black
1 business suit in a dark color (NO BLACK)
1 pair of khaki walking shorts
1 pair of jeans (not faded or torn)
1 conservative swim suit (boxer short type) — MODELS need a Speedo type
1 jogging suit
1 pair of clean white sneakers
1 brown and 1 black belt
Underwear and jock strap
Dress socks and casual socks

Hair brush
Body lotion, razor, shaving cream, soap, q-tips, kleenex, etc.

WOMEN: Khaki shirt
Oxford shirt in pastel colors
Lacoste or Izod type shirt in solid color
Khaki slacks in a polyester blend to prevent wrinkles
Tailored business suit with coordinated blouse with bow at the neck
Several pairs of stockings in all colors and neutral
Pumps in blue, brown, tan
Nude underwear and bras — a strapless bra, a body stocking
Evening dress — simple and elegant
Jeans — clean and hemmed
White sneakers
Walking shorts
Work-out leotard and stocking —
NO G-STRING TYPES
Hair brush
Makeup and accessories like Static Guard, clear polish, deodorant, lotion
Conservative one-piece swim suit
MODELS: mini skirt with matching blazer
HOT, HOT swim suit
Jewelry accessories — include a mock wedding band, mock pearls, various earrings, lots of hair bands, clips, etc.

PRACTICE COMMERCIALS

ONE-LINERS

The following commercial copy gives you examples of the different types of commercials you will encounter in auditions. There are one-liners, male and female spokespersons, a storyboard and several two person scenes. Work on each until you have interpreted it just exactly the way you think it should be. Then, think of another way to do it. Be prepared to read one-liners three different ways.

Gal: This peanut butter is "smoooother!"

Guy: How do I relax? At a "Samson Sauna Spa."

Gal: My cleaner cleans faster.

Guy: The difference in my "jeans." They stretch.

Gal: It has a fresh, new smell.

Guy: I like it, and I can afford it.

Gal or Guy: The way I get treated here, you'd think I owned the place.

Gal or Guy: (Taking picture) Smile! Got it!

Gal or Guy: Wow! That's a real surprise.

SIMPLE SCRIPTS

Woman: (at home at her telephone)

Flowers are a very important part of my life. They lift my spirits and make me smile. That's why I always give flowers as gifts. I call "Posies Unlimited," at 800-321-1234 and make my selection by phone. I ask for the "smile of the month" special. Why don't you?

Man: (in front of "Neighborhood Bank")

Quick. That's the most important service you can give me at a bank. That's why I bank at "Neighborhood," the fast service bank.

I never seem to have much time for deposits or withdrawals. I'm either on a lunch break or on my way to or from work. Neighborhood Bank caters to me. Gets me out fast, with special service, too. Oh, yes! I got a personal answer from the Vice President to my suggestion placed in Neighborhood's suggestion box. A speedy reply! Give Neighborhood a try.

Woman: (with small child)

Neurofibromatosis is a genetic disease that causes unpredictable tumor growth of the brain, skin, bones and internal organs. Neurofibromatosis strikes without warning. At 5 years, Jeanne has endured 4 major operations and months in a full body cast in her "fight for life" against this genetic time bomb. Together we can offer hope for the thousands of infants, children and adults suffering from Neurofibromatosis. Please call the NF Center today!

Man or Woman:

Last year I couldn't read this newspaper! . . . Oh, I'm not alone, there are thousands like me. I couldn't even fill out a job application. Adult Education has turned my life around. I've learned to read and write, and now I'm going for my high school diploma.

AUDIO-VISUAL SCRIPTS

Woman in Kitchen

Video	Audio
Tight shot of 3 cups on tray whisked away one at a time by 3 different hands.	No sound.
Cut to medium shot of woman right near table.	WOM: (On camera) There we go again. As fast as I fix Cocoa . . . it disappears. No matter when . . . morning, noon or night! But, I suppose it's no wonder . . .
Holds up package on word cue "Mother's."	Mother's, the most delicious hot cocoa. I enjoy Mother's hot cocoa every day . . . sort of between sweeping and sewing. A cocoa break certainly relaxes you. And my youngsters . . . well, they have Mother's, first thing in the morning . . .

and then first thing after school.

Move forward with her as she walks to bar, taking package with her. We see hand with spoon about to go into package . . . at this point . . .

And, I often pack Mother's cocoa in their lunchboxes. It's so easy!

(Voice-over) Mother's fixes instantly.

Close up of package.

(Voice-over) It's from Mother's and makes the best chocolate!

Man in Grocery Store

Video	Audio
Exterior shot. Zoom to interior. Meat Manager is very friendly. Non-threatening guy. Not aggressive.	
Walking down meat case, straightening packages.	I bet I go over this meat case 10 times a day to make sure everything is right.
Bring zoom in so the motion continues the scan of variety and brightness of the case is evident. Stop by service bell and push it.	But you know, this afternoon a lady I'd never seen before complained she couldn't find what she wanted. And she was right. So I showed her how to use this service bell. She says, "I'm afraid to bother you."
Uses hand motion to indicate non-assertive customer.	
Manager shrugs and delivers very sincere line.	So I said, "Forget bother, I'd like to think Grocery Mart has got what you want . . . choice of variety, choice of price." "Let me help you . . .
Motions toward case. Long shot for depth. Close up. Points to self — points to camera. Close with sig and jingle.	If I miss something in my meat case, tell me. I don't want to miss YOU as a customer."

Girl in Office

Video	Audio
Answers phone, talks to the side.	. . . . Carpet?
This will be a sequence of shots of the businesses in town that have dealt with CM, with a super card keyed in over each shot. Girl in office hangs up phone and talks to cam.	When big business in Atlanta needs carpet, they call Carpet Magic. Carpet Magic has earned a reputation second to none for quality and service for both business and home. Carpet Magic is one of Atlanta's largest dealers, and features quality Robert's Carpets . . . but for three days only (Carpet Magic) will sell all residential inventory for $8.88. With values to $23.95. All for just $8.88.
This Weekend Only May 27, 28, 29. $8.88 per yard. 2180 Emerson Street. ANIMATED LOGO SOUND ON.	LOGO TAG

Husband and Wife in Kitchen

Video	Audio
Open on woman sitting at kitchen table. She's got a broken arm in a sling. She's looking at food section in paper. Her husband comes through the kitchen door with two sacks full of groceries. He sets them down between woman and camera and leaves.	HUS: Hi, honey, I'm back from the grocery store. WOM: Yeah . . . I'm afraid to look. HUS: Relax, I shopped at Grocery Mart. I really saved us a lot of money, too. Go ahead . . . look what I bought . . . A 49-ounce Tide Detergent for just $1.49. WOM: Not bad. Not bad at all. HUS: And I saved $3 on this 6-pound ham. It was just 89 cents a pound. WOM: Gee . . . I couldn't have done better. HUS: That's not all. I also got two 16-ounce cans of Swanson peas for $1.39.
Cut to her husband setting two more sacks beside her. Cut to tighter shot of man adjusting woman's sling.	WOM: Aw, hon, you did good! HUS: Just a lucky break.

Husband and Wife at Kitchen Table

Video	Audio
Open on husband and wife at kitchen table.	Stan: Hon, what coffee did you switch to? This is the best cup of coffee I've had in a long time.
Wife crosses to stove, gets pot and returns to table.	Sue: It's not the coffee. It's the pot. This "Perky Pot" that Helen gave us as an anniversary gift — she said it would make the difference.
Pouring himself another cupful.	Stan: What a difference. I always thought it was the coffee that created the good flavor.
She lifts cup toward her lips, looking at "Perky Pot."	Sue: Just goes to show you. We've been shown . . . by "Perky Coffee Pot." And, oh yes, Helen's showmanship.

COMBINATIONS

On the Golf Course

Joe: Your game may not be improved, but you sure look better.

Jim: I'm shopping better.

Joe: Shopping better?

Jim: Yep. I'm going to the right place. The "Good Golfer's Store." It's specialized clothes only for the golfer. Tremendous selection at the price.

Joe: Good deal, I'll try them, too. Now, what are you going to do about your game?

At the Market

Jane: Excuse me, why are you buying "Easy Cleaner" instead of the one on sale?

Joan: The name says it all. It's "Easy."

Jane: What do you mean?

Joan: I do all the cleaning myself. No help. So, I'll spend more if it makes cleaning easy. "Easy Cleaner" is all the help I need.

Jane: "Easy Cleaner" . . . You're right. It's worth a few cents more — when it works.

Video		Audio
Middle-aged woman sits at table, paying bills. She is a little heavy and the domineering type. She looks off camera and yells to husband.		WOM: "Dom's Hair Styling, Ralph?"
Woman looks at next bill as she puts the first one down like it's hot. Yells at husband in same motion.		"A bush jacket! You, Ralph?"
Woman rolls eyes, shakes head, smiles as she writes checks. CU of Central Carolina Bank Check	 	ANNCR (VO): For unexpected expenses, it's nice to have Central Carolina Bank's overdraft plan, Silent Partner. The Silent Partner overdraft plan lets you write a check for more than you have in the bank. And no bank offers all the checking services CCB does.
Woman picks up another bill and looks aghast. Starts to dash into room where husband is. Woman is yelling.		WOM: "Nann's Naughty Negligee. Who is she, Ralph?"

Woman meets meek-looking husband. His hair is stylized and he wears a new suit. He hands his wife her new nightgown.

SUPER: CCB. We have a lot that other banks don't.

ANNCR (VO): CCB. We have checking services that other bank's don't.

AGENTS

Name: _____

Company: _____

Address: _____

Phone: _____

Name: _____

Company: _____

Address: _____

Phone: _____

Name: _____

Company: _____

Address: _____

Phone: _____

Name: _____

Company: _____

Address: _____

Phone: _____

Name: _____

Company: _____

Address: _____

Phone: _____

Name: _____

Company: _____

Address: _____

Phone: _____

Name: _____

Company: _____

Address: _____

Phone: _____

AUDITIONS

Company: _____

Product: _____

Agent: _____

Location: _____

Time/Date: _____

Company: _____

Product: _____

Agent: _____

Location: _____

Time/Date: _____

Company: _____

Product: _____

Agent: _____

Location: _____

Time/Date: _____

Company: _____

Product: _____

Agent: _____

Location: _____

Time/Date: _____

Company: _____

Product: _____

Agent: _____

Location: _____

Time/Date: _____

ABOUT THE AUTHOR

Iris Acker is not an ordinary actress. In fact, extraordinary doesn't even describe her ability. She has not only gained much success as an actress in theater, motion pictures, and television, but she also devotes a great deal of her time to teaching and coaching young actors and actresses trying to break into the business. One of her more famous students, Nancy Stafford, is the co-star of the television series, *Matlock*.

Iris places a great deal of emphasis on television commercials for her up and coming students. This book combines her many years of hands-on experience acting in commercials with her unique ability to communicate knowledge to others. Her students have profited greatly from her expertise, and with appearances in hundreds of commercials, she is certainly more than qualified to author a book on this subject.

Iris is a native of New York City, and currently resides in Miami, Florida. She is the producer and host of *On Stage With Iris Acker*, which appears on WLRN-TV 17, a Miami public broadcasting station. She is also involved with training and coaching actors and actresses for roles on stage, screen, and television.

Iris' professional achievements include appearances in numerous theater productions in New York and Florida. She has had principal roles in the films *Cocoon II*, *Flight of the Navigator*, *The Pilot*, *Intimate Strangers*, and *Whoops Apocalypse*. She has appeared in the daytime dramas *The Guiding Light*, and *Another World*. Iris counts, among her most successful achievements, the appearances in over 250 television commercials. She has done ads for "every airline there is," electric companies, major supermarkets, and drugstore chains. Her services as an actress and spokesperson are in constant demand. Most recently, Ms. Acker appeared with Joe Dimaggio in a Mr. Coffee commercial, and as Judge Mary Laverty on the TV series *Wiseguy*.